T0067819

Fish
Tales

and More . . .

Debbie Miley

WESTBOW
PRESS®
A DIVISION OF THOMAS NELSON
& ZONDERVAN

WestBow Press books may be ordered through booksellers or by contacting:

WestBow Press
A Division of Thomas Nelson & Zondervan
1663 Liberty Drive
Bloomington, IN 47403
www.westbowpress.com
1 (866) 928-1240

ISBN: 978-1-5127-8871-6 (sc)

Print information available on the last page.

WestBow Press rev. date: 06/15/2017

CONTENTS

IN APPRECIATION

It is greatly appreciated the help and encouragement which has been given regarding this project. Several people have looked at the drafts and offered their opinions and enjoyment of the characters involved in the skits. There have been those who offered help in editing of the material. They have offered their assistance in making a more polished piece. And, of course, I give my thanks to my Lord and Savior as He has encouraged me and directed my writing. Without Him, I am nothing.

DEDICATION

This book is dedicated to those who use the contents as a way to present the Bible to children so they might experience God for themselves and have the opportunity to accept Christ as Lord and Savior. It is also dedicated to the ones working in a very important ministry - children. May this prove to be a springboard for young people to begin their adventure of serving God. Have fun and learn to use the creativity God has given you. Listen to His voice and follow as He leads. And, of course, may the use of these skits be for furthering the kingdom of God.

MUCH ADO ABOUT NOTHING
Luke 10:38-42

The teacher has settled down in the chair with Bible on his/her lap. Welcomes the kids and begins to discuss something from the Bible when . . .. There is banging, chairs being moved roughly, muttering, etc. The curtain of the puppet theater is hit and ruffles back and forth. More muttering. A squawk every so often.

ALL OF A SUDDEN SCARVES, SOCKS, A BOOK AND OTHER THINGS START TO FLY OUT ABOVE THE PUPPET THEATER! (Just over the edge so as not to hit any of the kids.)

TEACHER: What on earth? Matilda? (No real response, just more commotion, muttering and a few squawks.)

TEACHER: Matilda? (Louder noises and a shoe box comes flying out.)

TEACHER: MATILDA!!!!

Matilda comes into view with a sock draped across her head, which she gives a fling and sends the sock flying.

MATILDA: WHAT!!?? (Said with agitation in the tone.)

The teacher looks at Matilda in silence for a little while.

TEACHER: Why are you making all of this noise and causing such a ruckus? You should be in Sunday School.

MATILDA: In Sunday School? With this mess? Look at it. Just look at it!!!!

TEACHER: Well, there isn't that much to straighten up and it can be done afterwards you know.

MATILDA: I have been making beds, washing dishes, picking up after everyone this morning. And now look at this mess! She reaches down and grabs a rag and gives it a hefty toss out into the audience. Where is everyone else? In Sunday School. There is so much work to be done and only one of me. Do you see them? There they are. Having all kinds of fun and not one of them has offered to help me. NOT ONE!

TEACHER: Now calm down Matilda. I am sure they will help when they are out of church. Which is where you should be right about now? You know, there is a story in the Bible which we are told about. It is almost this same situation. Let me tell you that story.

MATILDA: The Bible has a story about MWAH! You are kidding!

TEACHER: No, the Bible does have a story which is very similar to what you are going through right now. He cares that much about you that He included stories which will help you to work through Him to solve problems you have today.

MATILDA: Cool. Well, let's hear it.

TEACHER: Jesus had friends who were close to Him and with whom He could relax and just have a good time. His life on earth included all aspects of life. He lived a life very similar to ours. He had a job, He was a carpenter. He shared about God everywhere. He had friends. He had sad times in His life and happy times also.

MATILDA: I never thought of Jesus like that before. So He knows what it is to live His life just like us? Just like me?

TEACHER: That's right.

These friends were two sisters and a brother. They lived together in the same house where Jesus would come and relax and rest. Their names were Mary, Martha and Lazarus.

Martha was a really great hostess. She would spend days before a dinner party preparing the house, the menu, shopping for the food, doing early preparations. She had the best decorations, the plumpest pillows, top notch things which made her guests feel like royalty and pampered.

MATILDA: Now, that is a girl after my own heart. (Matilda is primping the curtain of the puppet theater.)

TEACHER: Martha was preparing a really special dinner party. Jesus and His apostles were coming to visit and stay for a few days in town. She wanted everything to be perfect because it was Jesus.

MATILDA: I can understand where that sister is coming from!

TEACHER: She was hurrying around the day of the dinner party. She had gotten up very early and had started getting things laid out and had started getting the many chores of the day going. She had some servants in to help in the many, many preparations. (Attention is shifted to the second, larger puppet theater.)

MARTHA: Mary! Did you slice those tomatoes and tear apart enough lettuce? How are the loaves of bread coming? Here! (She hands a sack with even more food to a worker.) Give this to Mary. Are there enough plates set out? Have you drawn enough water? (The puppets in the larger puppet theater are busy but not talking.)

TEACHER: As you can see, Martha is very organized and has a lot going on. The day has progressed and the evening meal is beginning. But there seems to be a lot of activity with food being passed out. Jesus and His apostles along with Lazarus are starting to eat and seem to be quite involved in different conversations. There is a lot of activity and laughter.

And there is Martha, still bustling. Still preparing food. She suddenly stops and begins to look around . . .

MARTHA: Mary? Where are you? Mary! She is never to be found to help me. She leaves all of this work for me to do by myself. SO! Does she think that these sandwiches and cakes are going to make and serve themselves? The lettuce, I suppose, is just going to lie down on a slice of bread on its own. . . (muttering) . . . MARY!

MATILDA: Martha is really getting worked up isn't she? She needs a chill pill about now. Her head is going to pop off and start rolling across the floor if she isn't careful.

The teacher looks thoughtfully at Matilda.

TEACHER: Hmmmmm. That is a very interesting comment, Matilda.

MATILDA: Well, Mary was helping her all day, after all. She wasn't left to do it all. Besides, she is fixing way too much. Keep telling the story.

TEACHER: Martha was really beside herself and she was becoming rather short. She is still preparing and working hard. She stands and looks around in the other room and then she stops cold . . . with her mouth wide open. Right there in front of Jesus listening to every word is . . .

MARTHA: Mary! There is that lazy girl. Sitting there among all those men laughing and talking with them. And she just lets me do all of this work. Well, I will show her.

TEACHER: Martha marches over to where Jesus is and begins to speak rather imploringly and without any hesitation.

MARTHA: Jesus. Are you enjoying yourself? Do you need anything? (She fusses with a few towels not looking at him directly.)

JESUS: No. No. Thank you so much, Martha. Again, everything was excellent. I am full and satisfied. Come sit down. (Martha is faltering and stammering as she begins.)

MARTHA: Well, that is something I would like to discuss with you. You know, it takes a lot of planning, shopping and preparing for all of this. It just doesn't happen on its own. Now, don't get me wrong. I don't mind doing this and especially for you. But like I said . . .

MATILDA: Is she kidding? Is she actually saying this to Jesus? Is she actually complaining like that?

The teacher just looks at Matilda and continues.

MARTHA: . . . all of this does not just happen by itself. I have worked hard for days getting this ready. And here sits Mary. She is letting me do all of this by myself . . .

JESUS: Martha. Martha. Come sit with me. You are getting all upset over nothing.

MARTHA: Jesus, surely you do not see the importance of this work. I am tired and I have a lot more work to do in cleaning up and preparing for the meals for tomorrow. And

Mary is just sitting here when she could be helping me get all of this done.

JESUS: Martha, you have prepared enough food to feed an army for days. You are fretting over things which will find their way to the garbage in the morning. Mary is spending time with me because she realizes that I am not going to be with you all before long. She is taking advantage of our time together. All of this will wait and be here when I am gone. My time with you and our friendship is what is of most importance. Come sit with me so I may enjoy our time together. You need to put away all of that which interferes with our relationship. I appreciate your work and all that you do. But I desire your company more. Come sit with me.

MATILDA: (She is sitting there with head hung down somewhat.) Wow! Martha is me, isn't she? I need to not worry so much about how things look or how people see me, the hostess with the mostess. I need to learn to spend time with Jesus and enjoy being with Him, right?

TEACHER: That's right Matilda. It is fine to have a clean, nice house. It is okay to prepare the best you can for friends and family. But don't let that get in the way of being able to enjoy your time with them and don't compromise your time with Jesus. Pick those things which are the most important. You still have time to join your friends at Sunday School.

MATILDA: OH! Yes! Sunday School. I just have time. See you there.

NOTES

LUNCH IS SERVED!
John 9:5-13

HARLEY is standing by himself and seems to be quite occupied with a lunch bag. He keeps reaching in and rearranging things.

HARLEY: One, two, three. Okay. And one, two. Everything seems to be here. I have my drink. I have my napkin. I am all set.

The teacher comes over and looks in the lunch bag.

TEACHER: That looks like a really good lunch, Harley.

HARLEY: OH! It is a really good lunch, ___(teacher's name)___. It is my favorite lunch ever. Fish sandwiches! I can almost taste them now.

TEACHER: That sounds really good!

HARLEY: I can hardly wait until lunchtime. I am hungry right now!!

TEACHER: Do you know how many people 3 loaves and 2 fish can feed?

HARLEY: One very hungry boy named HARLEY!

TEACHER: (Laughs) Well you are right. But did you know that it fed 5,000 men? Now that is not counting their families which could make it at least 10-15,000.

HARLEY: No way!

TEACHER: Not only that, but they ended up with 12 baskets of leftovers!

HARLEY grabs his head and shakes it from side to side.

HARLEY: I just can't imagine that. That's a lot of hungry people!

He looks in his lunch bag again.

HARLEY: Do you mean we could do that with my lunch?

TEACHER: Well, it happened once before.

HARLEY: How?

TEACHER: In the Bible it tells how three loaves of bread and 2 fish were multiplied to do just that.

HARLEY: For real?

HARLEY: How did it happen?

TEACHER: Well, let's settle back and I will tell you the story.

HARLEY sets his lunch bag to the side and settles back to hear the story.

TEACHER: Jesus had been teaching the people about God and how they were to live to please God. He had been doing this all day. Towards the end of the day, He and the whole crowd had made their way out into the countryside.

HARLEY: That makes me hungry just thinking about doing all of that walking and listening all day long. I'll bet they were tired and hungry. I'm hungry and I haven't walked anywhere!

TEACHER: (Laughing.) You are right HARLEY. They were tired and hungry. But no one had brought any food to eat along the way. Jesus' disciples were concerned because they were a long way from town, it was late and there was no food. So they went to Jesus to see what they needed to do.

HARLEY: Wow! That's a hard one. What happened?

TEACHER: The disciples went to Jesus and told him: 'Jesus. We really have a big problem here. There are so many people who have followed us here listening to You as You taught. They are very tired and hungry. But it is a long way from town and what on earth are we going to feed them?'

Jesus had finished his teaching and was relaxing a bit chatting with different ones of the crowd. He said, 'Well, feed them.'

HARLEY: Feed them? How could they possibly feed all of those people?

TEACHER: The disciples looked at each other and probably didn't say anything for a while. Jesus asked them if there was any food at all. They said they had found someone who had brought a lunch of 3 loaves of bread, probably buns or rolls of some kind, and 2 fish. He told them, 'Go get it and bring it here.' And that is what they did.

HARLEY: I don't think I can give up my wonderful lunch. (He looks in at his lunch bag again.) I really like my sandwiches.

TEACHER: Well, whoever this was, they gave up their lunch to help someone out. So the disciples took this lunch back to Jesus. Can you imagine what they were thinking?

HARLEY: Yeah! Jesus is one crazy dude! *Harley looks out at the audience and opens his mouth and is bobbing his head as he is laughing.*

TEACHER: Okay, Harley. It does sound crazy. But wait until you hear what happens. Jesus had all of the people sit down where they were at so they could pass out the food in an orderly manner. Then when everyone was quiet and watching to see what Jesus was going to do, He took the 3 loaves and 2 fish and lifted them up so everyone could see and asked that the food would be blessed. Then He handed them to the disciples and asked that they pass them out to everyone. After the food had been passed out and everyone had had their fill, He asked the disciples if everyone was done. Then they were instructed to take 12 baskets and pick up all of the leftovers. All twelve baskets were filled to the top.

HARLEY: Wow! (*He looks in his lunch bag again.*) All that food from just 3 loaves and 2 fish. Can you imagine?

TEACHER: Pretty fantastic, huh?

HARLEY: That is really neat. But one thing. Jesus knew the disciples could not get enough food to feed all of those people. And weren't they poor? They didn't have enough money to buy that much food. Why didn't Jesus just make hamburgers and ham & cheese sandwiches appear?

TEACHER: Harley, God often asks us to do things which are pretty fantastic and simply out of our reach to do.

HARLEY: That sounds kind of mean.

TEACHER: Not at all. If we did things which we could do without God, we would never learn how much He cares for us. We would never learn to have faith in Him for those really tough times we all have in our lives – like the bully out on the play ground, that hard spelling or math test we are going to have this week, or having to say we are sorry for something we have done which is wrong or has hurt someone else. If we do just those things we can do ourselves we will never learn how truly wonderful and powerful God truly is.

HARLEY: So, God wants us to turn to Him for everything? Even a fish sandwich for lunch?

TEACHER: That's right. God cares very much for you and for me. He wants to help us, He wants us to walk with Him each day. That is why He sent Jesus to die on the cross for us. Jesus came so we can learn about God and how He wants us to live.

HARLEY: He really is a neat God, isn't He?

TEACHER: Harley, it is lunch time.

HARLEY: Oh boy! I can finally eat my favorite lunch ever!

Harley grabs his lunch bag and begins to exit but stops and turns around.

HARLEY: _____teacher's name_____, would you like to share my lunch?

TEACHER: Why how nice Harley. I think I will. Thank you.

NOTES

THE FIRST CRUISE LINER
Genesis 6:1-8:22

TEACHER: We have a good story to learn about today. How many of you know what a flood is? (Pause to give them time to answer.) There is a story in the Bible . . . (In the background a cawing like that of a crow can be heard.)

CAW! CAW! CAW! (The teacher looks around. Then . . .)

TEACHER: Did you hear that? (Give the children a chance to answer and/or make comments in reply.)

CAW! CAW!

TEACHER: Now I know I heard a crow. Did you kids?

CAW! CAW! (Out comes Hector. He sets himself down next to the teacher with his legs hanging over the side of the table where she is sitting. Let him preen himself for a while. The crow looks over the kids in front of him and then turns and looks at the teacher.)

TEACHER: Oh, Hector! Kids, I want you to meet Hector the crow!

HECTOR: CAW! Hi kids. I am really glad to meet you. (Hector takes a bow as he is sitting there.)

TEACHER: I am so glad you have come, Hector. You can help me tell about the event from the Bible called the Great Flood. Do you remember that one? Did Noah come with you?

HECTOR: CAW! Do I remember? I'll say I do. My dad and mom used to tell us kids all about it. It is one of my favorite family adventures. And Noah did come. CAW!

NOAH: (Noah comes into view.) Hi kids! Hi, __(teacher's name)___.

TEACHER: Hi Noah! It is so good to have you here with us.

NOAH: I'm glad to be here with you and all you kids!

TEACHER: (To Hector.) Now, didn't you say there is some family connection for you?

HECTOR: CAW! I'll say. You see, I am a crow. One of my ancestors, cousin Rufus Raven, was on that ark. And God used him. That is so neat. CAW!

TEACHER: Why don't both of you start at the beginning of the story and let the kids know what happened which brought on the flood and finally your ancestor's involvement?

HECTOR: CAW! I sure will. Settle back kids. This is a true story. Now way back in the way back machine, CAW, God was looking at the world and how man was doing. It really made Him sad, caw (a soft caw).

NOAH: That's right. He actually was sorry that he had made man. Men and women were not paying any attention to Him and they were being really bad. They did whatever they wanted without thinking about their neighbor or the guy down the street and how it would affect them.

HECTOR: Caw (another soft caw). It---it really hurt God's heart. Caw. (Hector moves his head from side to side as he looks down.)

TEACHER: (To the kids.) Did you know we can hurt God's heart?

HECTOR: CAW! We can.

NOAH: Then God told me, "I am going to blot out man whom I created. And not only will I destroy man, but I will destroy the animals. the creeping things and even the birds of the sky."

HECTOR: CAW! CAW! That is terrible. God said He was sorry He ever made them. (Soft caw). Now God was looking at the terrible things people were doing and how bad they had become. But He began to watch a particular man. This man's name was Noah. HIM! (Hector puts a wing on Noah's shoulder.) Now, Noah was a righteous man.

TEACHER: (To the kids.) Does anyone know what righteous means? (Give time for the kids to answer.) Righteous means you are more than just a good person. It means you are trying to follow God and listen to all He says.

HECTOR: CAW! That is right. Noah loved God and followed God in everything he did. (Noah nods his head in agreement.) Noah had found favor in God's eyes. God approved of how Noah tried to live his life for Him. Noah walked daily with God. You can do the same by reading His word and praying to Him. CAW!

NOAH: One day as God and I were talking, God said, "Noah, I am going to destroy all of the men on earth and the animals and the plants. I am doing this because the men of the earth have become so very bad and they hurt each other and they do not follow me or look for me like you and your family do. So I want you to build an ark. There will be rooms in it and when you make it, you will coat it inside and outside with pitch.

TEACHER: (To the kids.) Pitch is tar. It is a sticky black substance. When it dries, it is very hard and it will seal out water. So by coating the ark on the outside and the inside, it will make it water tight, which means no water will come into the boat. It will float.

HECTOR: CAW! That is right. So God gave the building instructions to Noah. The ark was going to be very large and it was going to have three decks or three floors. Each deck would have rooms. He told Noah to build the ark so the door was in the side of it where all the animals and birds would enter. And there was a window and opening on the top which could be opened and removed. CAW!

NOAH: Now the people had never seen an ark before. They all came by to watch my sons and me work. They just came to make fun of us. It hurt a lot. (Have two or three male puppets to ask questions of Noah.) First one would ask, "Hey, Noah! What are you doing?" "I'm building an ark." "What is an ark?" "It is something which will hold a lot of animals and my family and it floats on water." "Why? Why do you need something to float on water?" "Do you see any water?" "I don't see any water that needs something like that." People continued to make fun of my sons and me. They would say to each other, "Let's go watch Crazy Noah build his ark!" "Hey! Noah! Who told you to build this?! "God told me to build the ark." "And why did He tell you to build the ark, Crazy Noah?" "He said He was sorry He made man because they do not pay any attention to Him nor follow Him." "OOOOO! I am so afraid! OOOOO!"

HECTOR: Noah kept building the ark as God had commanded Him.

NOAH: "Now, Noah," God told me, "I am going to bring the water down to flood the entire earth and destroy all of life. And I am going to make a covenant with you that you and your family, your wife and your three sons and their wives, will be able to enter into the ark and I am going to protect you and save you. This is because you are a righteous man."

HECTOR: CAW!

TEACHER: Do any of you know what a covenant is? (Wait for the kids.) It is a promise, but even stronger than a promise. It is a promise which can never be broken. God cannot break a promise or He would not be God. God is perfect.

HECTOR: CAW! That is right. Now here is a really neat part. CAW! God told Noah to get the animals together. They will come here and you must be gathering the food which is edible for them and for you and your family so all will live. Now there will be two of every kind. There will be a male and a female. That would be lions and tigers and bears! Oh my. CAW! You will have a boy lion and a girl lion. And the same for all the others. Two snakes, two turtles, two kangaroos. Animals of all kinds, insects of all kinds and birds of all kinds. CAW! I sure wish I could have heard what the people's comments were and seen their faces as tigers and bears and giraffes and others all came on their own and boarded the ark on their own. CAW! Wouldn't you?

NOAH: Finally, God said to me, "Noah, it is time for you to enter into the ark with your family. You have gathered all from the animal world I told you to. You have gathered all of the food you will need. Everything is ready for your salvation. In seven days I am going to start the rain. It is going to rain for forty days and forty nights."

HECTOR: CAW! So Noah did what God said. They arranged the last of the animals and made sure they were comfortable and the last of the food was put in place. Then he got his family together and they took one last look at the world as they had known it up until then. As they got in, God closed the door of the ark and made sure the seams were water tight on the outside and Noah and his sons took care of the inside.

After the door was closed and sealed and seven days had gone by, it began to really rain. And did it rain? CAW! CAW! CAW! It rained for forty days and forty nights without stopping. The ark floated away on top of the water. What an experience! It rained so much that the tallest of all the mountains on the earth were covered with water. And not just a little bit. There was no place to stand. Everything that was alive on the earth was destroyed. Only the creatures inside the ark and Noah and his family survived. CAW! CAW! CAW!

NOAH: And after forty days and forty nights, it finally stopped raining. All of that water remained for a very long time, 150 days! That is five months.

God remembered us and everyone and everything which was with us on the ark. So God caused a wind to blow over the earth and all of that water. The water began to subside or go away. It gathered into what we call oceans, lakes, ponds, rivers, brooks and so on.

That took five months to happen. Then two months later, that makes it seven months, on the seventeenth day of the seventh month, the ark came to rest on the mountains of Mount Ararat. The water continued to go away into the tenth month. The tops of the mountains could be seen now easily.

HECTOR: CAW! Noah waited 40 more days and he opened up the window which God had him build into the ark. When he opened the window, this is where my cousin Rufus comes in. Noah took Rufus and released him into the air. Cousin Rufus flew back and forth across the waters. He flew until the land showed up again and had become dry again. CAW! We crows and ravens can fly for a very long time. Plus we can walk on land kinda like people. So cousin Rufus could land on the mountain tops and stay okay. CAW!

NOAH: Now, I took a dove and released her to see if she would return or find a place to land and stay. She came back because there were no trees for her to land in. I waited seven days and then released her again. She was gone all day and towards evening she came back and she had a freshly broken off olive leaf to give to me. I was very hopeful then. So after another seven days I released the dove. But this time she did not come back. The dry land was almost back and there was grass with trees growing and God was replenishing the plant life to the earth for the animals and Noah and his family. After one more month, God told me to release the animals and all of the creatures and the birds. He said that he and his family could come out of the ark now as the earth was ready to be lived on once again.

HECTOR: CAW! Now there were not the same numbers of animals which left the ark as had gotten onto the ark. They now had babies and each animal family left the ark together. CAW! After all the animals left the ark, Noah took his family and they built an altar out of stones and offered burnt offerings to God. They were so happy and thankful that God had saved them and had redone the earth after the flood.

CAW! CAW! CAW! Isn't that cool?

TEACHER: It was great to hear about your cousin Rufus from so long ago.

HECTOR: CAW! And it shows how much God really loves us. Even when we don't do what our parents tell us to do or we are mean to someone or we tell a lie or take something that belongs to someone else, we hurt God's heart and make Him very sad. But He made a way to save us all. He sent His Son, Jesus, to earth to live and to die for all the things we do wrong. We can ask for forgiveness for everything we do wrong. He then cleans our heart. It will all be new.

NOAH: Isn't that fantastic? God loves you very much.

HECTOR: CAW! CAW! CAW!

NOTES

BEACHFRONT PROPERTY
Matt 7:24-27

Have some recordings of hammering, sawing, party sounds with music, laughter and talking. Also have the sound of "slapping" water. The sounds of wind and pounding rain will be needed also. These will be played in the background behind the teacher telling the story. The puppets will be acting out the story. They do not actually talk. They just act out the parts as their stories are told.

TEACHER: Sometimes when Jesus taught the people, He would tell stories to get His point across. You have heard this story I am certain. There were two men who wanted to build their houses close to the water. What kind of ground do you find close to the water?

Sand. Beaches. How many of you have been to a fresh water lake beach or to an ocean beach? Are beaches very stable? Could a house stand forever on sand? Why or why not?

(Give the children time to give their answers.)

Sand shifts a lot. There is no strong foundation for the house. Now these men looked around and they decided where they wanted to build their houses.

One man saw a grove of trees. The trees surrounded an open spot which was just big enough for a house and a small yard all around. It was tucked back away from being directly on the beach. It was protected from the wind and waves should they come up onto the beach during a storm. He found a very large rock which stuck out in front of where he wanted to build. After he did some digging back further, he found that the rock was very securely buried into the hillside.

"This will be perfect for the foundation for my building!" He was very excited and began to dig down so the supports of the house were not just sitting on the rock. Then he carved out ruts into the rock which would hold the supports for his house securely. It was very hard work and took a very long time.

In the background you can hear the sawing and hammering. This will continue until the first man's house is complete.

The second man watched the first man and decided he was doing way too much work and it would be a long time before he had a house. So this second man walked up and down the beach looking for the best view he could have. He wanted to hear the water hitting the beach and see the sun come up over the ocean. *(The sound of slapping water begins here for the second man.)* He wanted a panoramic view from anywhere in his house. So he started to put the supports for his house down in the sand where he thought it would be a good depth. He was so happy with his view.

The second man had his house done in a couple of weeks. He had friends down for cookouts and parties. They had a great time. Everyone was in great awe of the fantastic views. Off to the side you could hear banging and sawing going on. This continued for a few more weeks. The second man and all his friends would go up to see how the first man's house was coming along. The second man would tell him, "You should have come down where my house is. The views are unbelievable and you would have been done by now." The first man said in time his house would prove to be very worthy for him and his family. The second man would just laugh and return to his great views with his friends. The first man could hear them laughing and singing and playing. *(In the background laughter, music and talking can be heard.)* "My faithfulness will reward me one day." He would just return to working on his house.

Finally, the first man's house was complete. It was not as open or as close to the water and beach as the second man's house. He could open the windows and feel the breeze as it blew up to his house. He had a beautiful view of the ocean, the beach and the second man's house. They still were having their friends over to party and enjoy the views.

One day, the first man and his family were out on their front porch enjoying the day. He looked up and saw a great storm cloud coming across the ocean toward their beach. It was very dark and you could see lightening coming out of the clouds. He sent the family off to close all the shutters, gather up the food from the garden and gather up their toys, furniture and tell the workers to gather their things also and to get into the house. He went down to the second man's house and told them about the storm cloud coming and to come up to his house for protection. They didn't see the urgency to leave the house.

The first man was sitting in the living room with his workers and family waiting for the storm to come. And it hit. The wind was very forceful. The rain was very heavy and pounded against the sides of his house, but it stood fast. It didn't as much as shudder from the force of the wind. The house stood fast.

As the storm continued, one of the workers told the man he could hear someone at the front door. The man went to the door and the second man stumbled in with his family and some of his friends. "The storm has destroyed my house. The waves were so mighty and high it caused my house to fall. I am unable to find some of my friends. We need shelter!" The first man got dry clothes for them all and found some warm broth and bread to eat. His family and workers started to console them and comfort them because of the terrible experience they had just gone hrough. They could still hear the storm going on outside, but his house stood strong.

The next morning after they had breakfast, they went out onto the porch to see what the storm had done. And just as the second man said, his house had been destroyed. It had fallen flat. There was nothing left, just as if it had never been there.

Crying loudly, "Why hadn't I listened? Why hadn't I believed the words spoken and built my house on the rock? This is terrible, so terrible." It was very hard to comfort him and his family and his remaining friends.

You see the second man raise his hands in the air as he looks at the sky. Then he drops his hands to his face and begins to sob.

This experience is what Jesus was telling the people during the time He was on Earth. He told them how they should live. He told them how they needed to listen to what He had to say and to believe him. But just like these two men, some listen and build their lives on what Jesus says and teaches. Some do not listen. They think they know the best way to do things. They build their lives on things which are not strong and are easily destroyed and they lose everything.

Jesus came to Earth as a tiny baby. He lived His life as an example for all of us. He honored God and lived by His principles. He then died on the cross to pay for our sin. Whenever you do something wrong; i.e., tell a story, are mean to someone to hurt them, do not obey your parents, take something that does not belong to you; that is all sin.

When you do that, you are disobeying God. Adults do the same thing. God knew we could not be perfect because we sin. God cannot stand sin. Sin cannot be where God is. You cannot be good enough. So, because God loves each one of us so much, He sent his son to die on the cross and raised Him the third day. When you want to be saved, you tell God that you are a sinner who cannot save himself and ask Him to save you. Only when we ask God to save us from our sin can we be saved. There is nothing else you can do to please God. You then live your life according to how He says you should.

If you have any questions, you can ask one of the teachers and they can explain more to you so you understand what and why you need to do this.

You can find this in Matthew 7:24-27. We can show you where to find it in your Bible.

NOTES

BREAKOUT!
Acts 16:16-34

TEACHER: Today we are going to hear about a time when Paul and Silas were jailed. There were accusations which were not completely true. They had cast a demon out of a slave girl. The ones who owned the slave girl were making money as they would show her before groups of people and charging them admission.

The slave girl would follow Paul & Silas around for several days.

SLAVE GIRL: (In a loud voice.) These men are the servants of the Most High God. They proclaim to us the way of salvation.

SILAS: Paul, what are we going to do about this slave girl who keeps following us? She is really becoming a disruption.

PAUL: I know. Her outbursts are very disruptive. We need to deal with that demon in her. She will be normal then and can be saved. Let's help her.

TEACHER: Paul and Silas turned towards the slave girl. They had become very annoyed with the spirit in her. So Paul said. . .

PAUL: I command you in the name of Jesus Christ to come out of her!

TEACHER: What do think happened? (*Give children time to discuss this.*) The spirit immediately left. The slave girl was now normal and Paul and Silas helped her to be saved.

Now, do you remember my telling you about those who owned her? They were watching all of this. They watched as the spirit left the girl and they saw the change in her. They were the ones who were upset and angry. They were so angry that they took hold of Paul and Silas and drug them to the market place where the authorities were. They no longer had a way to make money using this slave girl.

Standing before the magistrates (or the rulers) the two men began to tell the story. Now they didn't tell the truthful story to their audience. They told lies against Paul and Silas.

FIRST MAN: These two men we bring before you are Jews and they are bringing a great deal of trouble to our city! They are causing all kinds of problems.

SECOND MAN: They are teaching customs to us and we are Romans. These things they are teaching are not lawful for us to hear or practice.

TEACHER: The crowd which had gathered heard all of this and bean to become angry and upset. They were so angry they tore their clothes and rose up against Paul and Silas. The rulers commanded that Paul and Silas be beaten and then thrown into prison. The guards were told to be sure that they did not escape.

When the jailer received these orders he placed them into the inner part of the prison and placed their feet into stocks. (The jailer puts chains on Paul and Silas and leads them off stage.)

How do you think Paul and Silas handled all of these terrible things which happened to them? (Give the kids a chance to answer/discuss this.)

Well, they acted in a way completely not expected. The Bible tells us what happened . . . It was now midnight in the prison.

PAUL and SILAS: (Together.) "Praise God from Whom all blessings flow."

SILAS: Paul, isn't God good?

PAUL: He is. Oh, God. We know what a merciful God you are. You are so good to us. Thank you for your love and mercy you give to us.

SILAS: Oh yes, Lord. You are so mighty and good.

TEACHER: All of the other prisoners were listening to their singing and praying.

All of a sudden everything began to shake violently. They were having an earthquake! The very foundation of the prison shook. Then all of a sudden, all the doors in the prison flew open!

The jailer woke up suddenly from all the shaking and the prisoners were yelling. He knew he was in trouble when he saw all the cell doors were wide open. He just knew that all the prisoners had fled. He would be killed over this as his punishment; so he took out his sword to kill himself.

PAUL: (Said loud and earnestly.) Wait! Listen! Do not hurt yourself. Look around. We are still here.

JAILER: Bring me a torch or lamp.

TEACHER: He was handed a light immediately. He ran into Paul and Silas's cell and fell to his knees. He was trembling.

JAILER: Sirs, what must I do to be saved?

PAUL: Believe on the Lord Jesus Christ and you will be saved. You and your household.

TEACHER: The jailer brought Paul and Silas home with him and they told his family about Christ. They were saved also. With that, they all sat down and ate.

NOTES

JONAH AND CLARENCE
Book of Jonah

(Interviewer has clipboard and pen in hand. Finally looks up at audience and smiles.)

INTERVIEWER: We have a very interesting guest for you today. He has a lot to tell us of a very interesting event. Please give a warm welcome to Clarence, the Whale.

(Nothing happens. Total silence. Then a little louder.)

INTERVIEWER: Say hello to Clarence, the Whale.

(Interviewer looks out at the audience with a questioning look then turns to the curtained window. This time in a loud whisper. . .)

INTERVIEWER: Clarence? Are you there? We're ready for you. (Some more silence. Then a lot of loud throat clearing. A spraying of water into the audience.)

INTERVIEWER: Clarence? Clar-r-r-ence??! (Still no Clarence, but. . .)

CLARENCE: Uh-h-h-h-h-h! Me-me-me-me! (Slowly Clarence comes up and does some slow movements like he is swimming in place.)

CLARENCE: Uh, Hi everybody. I'm Clarence.

INTERVIEWER: Welcome Clarence. I understand you know quite a bit about a very important event. Can you tell us about it?

CLARENCE: Know about it? Know about it? I didn't get a choice in knowing about it. I wasn't even asked. I couldn't have gotten away from it if I had tried.

INTERVIEWER: Really? (Looks out at audience with an incredulous look.) Can you fill us in on it?

CLARENCE: Well, I was just finishing up my lunch of some fine octopi and wonderful squid. (Looks out at the audience.) Don't you just love a great lunch? OH! And man. When you get to that ink sac. . . (Looks upwards and moves head back and forth.) You bite into it and that warm black liquid runs between your lips. Yu-u-u-um!

(Quickly turns head back to the audience.)

Now those suction cups. Whew! I have quite a time with them. If one gets stuck on the roof of my mouth. . . WOW! (Looks back at the audience.) No hands, you know!

INTERVIEWER: Sounds like a wonderful lunch. (Turns to audience pointing at open mouth while making gagging noise.) Clarence!? Can we get back to the story?

CLARENCE: Oh! Sorry. I really like squid.

Well, like I said, I had just finished a good lunch of squid. I was actually taking a last bite when I swallowed something, but it wasn't squid! It had HAIR! (Looks back and forth at the audience.) It was yelling a lot and waving its tentacles, but there were no suction cups.

Then it started moving around inside of me. Back and forth. Back and forth. Back and forth.

(Exaggerated movement of head back and forth from one side of audience to opposite side.)

I finally yelled, "Will you stop?! Make it STO-O-O-OO-O-O-P!"

Then it started making a noise. At first I couldn't make it out. Then I heard it clearly. "Lord! Why?" Lord??! My name is Clarence, not Lord. And asking me "Why?"? I should be asking it why! Why was it in my lunch?

INTERVIEWER: So, who do you think it was talking to if not you?

CLARENCE: Well, I thought that very thing myself. Who is it talking to? But I didn't have to wonder long. Out of nowhere came, "Jonah, Jonah!" It answered, "Yes, Lord?" It was talking to the Lord.

INTERVIEWER: (Looking out at the audience and back at Clarence) You mean it was talking to God?

CLARENCE: Yep!

INTERVIEWER: And God was answering back?

CLARENCE: The one and only!

INTERVIEWER: How impressive!

CLARENCE: (Nodding his head several times.) Yep. Pretty impressive. So, I got kinda quiet and decided I would just listen for a while.

INTERVIEWER: What were they talking about?

CLARENCE: At first I didn't understand it all. Seems like God wanted Jonah to go to a group of people in a place called Nineveh. But Jonah wasn't wanting to go very badly. In fact, he ran from God. I had heard about these people from Nineveh. They were a very wicked group of people.

Well, Jonah bought a ticket on a boat and got on. He was going clear across the sea to a place called Tarshish. He thought that was it.

INTERVIEWER: You mean, Jonah ran away from God? He didn't obey Him?

CLARENCE: Yep, that about tells it all.

INTERVIEWER: So what happened then?

CLARENCE: Jonah had just settled down for his ride down below and had fallen asleep. He was sleeping really good! God was not very happy with Jonah. So he sent a storm. He caused the wind to make really big, really strong waves to toss the boat around.

The boat went up and down and back and forth. Up and down and back and forth. Up and down and back and forth. (Move head exaggeratedly in the directions given.)

INTERVIEWER: Are you okay Clarence? (Looking at Clarence with great concern. Clarence is kind of leaning to one side and moaning slightly.)

CLARENCE: Yep. I almost made myself seasick there.

Well, the captain and the crew were sure they were going to perish. They worshipped other gods. They had never worshipped God before then. Everyone was praying to their gods and nothing happened. The storm got really bad and they were really scared. Then the captain remembered Jonah. He saw he wasn't there with them. So he went below deck and found Jonah sleeping very soundly. He shook him and woke him up. He said, "Hey man! What are you doing? We are about to be destroyed in this storm. Get up and pray to your God and ask Him to stop it. Maybe your God will have mercy on us and not let us die."

All of the sailors got together on deck and said, "Let's draw straws to see who is responsible for this terrible thing happening to us. Then we can take care of him." So they drew straws and Jonah drew the short straw.

They all gathered around him and began to demand and ask questions of him all at once. "Who are you? Where do you come from? What do you do? From what group of people are you?"

Jonah stood up then and said, "My name is Jonah. I am a Hebrew and I worship the Lord, the God of heaven, who made the sea and the land."

Well, the men had heard of God and they were terrified then. They knew that Jonah must have done something terribly wrong. They knew Jonah was trying to run away from the Lord because the Lord had told them so.

The men turned to Jonah and asked, "What have you done? What should we do to you to make this storm stop?"

Jonah knew he was the cause of this frightening storm because of his rebellion against God and him not wanting to obey Him. So he told them, "Throw me into the sea. When you do, the storm will stop."

Well, the men did not want to do that to Jonah because they didn't want him to die. So they tried to row back to shore. But the storm became fiercer and stronger.

The boat went up and down and back and forth. Up and down and . . .

INTERVIEWER: (Puts hand out on top of Clarence.) Maybe you had better not do that. Remember last time?

CLARENCE: (Chuckles slightly.) Yeah, right!

The men began to pray to God then and to worship Him. They had no choice. They asked God to forgive them for throwing Jonah over to die. But the boat was going to be destroyed. And then they all would die. So they picked Jonah up and threw him overboard.

What do you suppose happened then? (Give the kids a chance to answer.)

Yep. Enter stage right, ME! Minding my own business eating some squid and G-U-L-P!

INTERVIEWER: So, that's the end of the story? That is the end of Jonah?

CLARENCE: Oh NO! For three days and three nights he paced back and forth in my belly. Jonah and God talking back and forth. I will tell you this much, I didn't get very much sleep. And I didn't eat anything for three days!

INTERVIEWER: What did they talk about?

CLARENCE: Well, Jonah told God how sorry he was for not obeying him. He told God how he understood how great

He is. And how even after he, Jonah, had disobeyed Him, God never left him and never forgot him. Jonah asked for forgiveness for his sin.

INTERVIEWER: What happened then?

CLARENCE: Jonah told God that salvation from our sins can only be found in Him. So Jonah said he would go to Nineveh and tell them how bad they were and how they needed to ask God for forgiveness.

And with all of that pacing and talking for three days and three nights and I hadn't slept and hadn't eaten, I wasn't feeling very well. I was up close to the shore by this time. Well, I couldn't help it. I lost it then. One big belch did it. The last I saw of Jonah he looked kinda slimy and he was walking toward Nineveh.

INTERVIEWER: Did you hear anything more of what happened?

CLARENCE: Well, some sea gulls landed on my back a few days later and said that the whole town of Nineveh heard how God knew how wicked they were and how they needed to ask Him for forgiveness. So the whole town did!

INTERVIEWER: Wow. That's quite a story. It kind of reminds me of our lives today. When our parents tell us to do something or our teachers, we really need to obey. We shouldn't ignore them, say no or run from them. We need to make sure we obey. Because you see, that is what God has told you boys and girls to do. He gave you an assignment just like Jonah. He told you to obey your mother and father. That is a good way for you to show you love them and that you love God. And when you don't obey, you ask for forgiveness and then do what you were asked. You ask your parents and you ask God to forgive you.

Clarence, thank you so much for clearing up what happened to Jonah

Tell Clarence good-bye kids!

CLARENCE: Good-bye, kids. Sure glad to have met you! BYE!!!

NOTES

LIES!
Genesis 3:1-24

TEACHER: Do you all know who Adam & Eve are? They were the first man and first woman ever. Their home was in the Garden of Eden. It was a perfect place in every way you can think. Beautiful flowers; lots of trees to climb; wide rolling meadows; and every kind of animal you can imagine. Even Adam and Eve were perfect. They had never done anything wrong. They had never sinned. It was quite common for Adam and Eve to walk together with God through this paradise just talking.

We have a visitor who is going to tell us what went on there. Her name is Jennie. You might say she will give us a bird's eye view. She is Jennie Robin.

JENNIE: Hi kids! How are all of you? Have you ever flown? You need to try it. It is grand. Oh, I don't see any feathers on any of you. That might not work very well.

TEACHER: Hi, Jennie. It is so good for you to come and help us know what went on with Adam and Eve.

JENNIE: I would love to. I remember them so well. They were some really nice people.

TEACHER: I told the kids how they used to walk through the Garden with God. They would talk together, the three of them, just spending the day together.

JENNIE: Let me take it from there. God was going over the names Adam had given to all the animals. He was showing them what was good to eat and how to take care of the plants. He showed them where the sweetest fruit was. Before long, they found themselves in front of a particular tree. God stopped here and said that Adam could have fruit from all the trees in the Garden except from this one. He could not eat the fruit from this one tree. The name of this tree was the Tree of Knowledge of Good and Evil. That was the only tree that God held back from them. There was so much good food available for them to eat.

TEACHER: That doesn't sound like it would be hard to do. So many choices. How hard could it be to bypass just the one tree?

JENNIE: It seemed like it would be an easy command to follow. But just wait. One day in the Garden, Adam and Eve were together and not doing too much. They must have been waiting for God to come so they could go walking again.

As it happened, they were standing close to the tree from which they could not eat the fruit. Then, they got the surprise of their short lives! The snake came up to them. He was a very tricky animal and he began his tricks on them. The snake went up to Eve. Adam was just a little ways off and could hear what was being said. The snake asked Eve a question, "Did God really tell you that you cannot eat from any tree in the Garden?"

TEACHER: Kids, is that what God said? (Give the kids time to come up with what God really said.) The snake is twisting what God said and he is making Eve question God. That can happen to us too. Friends can try to tell us something other than the truth.

JENNIE: That is exactly what he did. And remember that Adam was right there and did not say anything to help Eve. Eve answered the snake by saying, "We may eat fruit from the trees in the Garden, but God did say, 'You must not eat fruit from the tree that is in the middle of the Garden, and you must not touch it, or you will die.'"

TEACHER: Kids, did God say that? (Wait for the kids to answer.) What was it that God say? (Give the kids to remember what God said.) Eve added to what God actually said. The snake twisted what God said and Eve added to what He said. Were these things that are right to do?

JENNIE: What God says is truth. What He says does not need to be changed by twisting it or adding to it. But this is not over yet. There is still more, so listen carefully.

The snake answered Eve, "Heh-heh-heh! Oh Eve, Eve. You aren't going to die. God knows when you eat from this tree that you will be like Him. You will be able to recognize good and evil. It is a mind-expanding tree. You will gain great wisdom. Eve, Eve, Eve."

Eve listened to the snake and she looked at the tree. It was a beautiful tree. The fruit looked like it would be good to eat. It even smelled sweet just hanging there. She thought of the wisdom she would gain by just eating one piece of fruit. So, she reached up and pulled a piece of fruit from one of the lower branches. It felt cool in her hand. It was round and smooth and smelled so very sweet. It had a beautiful color also. Eve thought to herself, "How could something so beautiful be wrong for us to have?" She took a big bite of it and the juice ran down her chin. It was sweet and luscious. Far better than she could have imagined. Then she turned to Adam and gave it to him to have some. He reached out and took the fruit from her and took a bite also. It was good. He finished off the fruit and looked at Eve.

They began immediately to see things very differently. They looked at each other and they were shocked and ashamed as they realized they were naked. They did not have any clothes on! They immediately went into the bushes and began to sew leaves together to make themselves clothes to cover up their nakedness. They were so ashamed.

TEACHER: They did not have any problems being naked before because they did not notice. Have you ever done something wrong like lied, stolen something, disobeyed your parents? How did you feel afterwards? How did it make you act? What did you do when you were asked about it? Jennie is going to tell us how Adam and Eve handled their disobedience to God.

JENNIE: Adam and Eve had just finished sewing the leaves together and slipped into their clothes when down the path of the Garden they could hear God coming towards them. They were scared because of what they had done. They jumped back into the bushes and crouched down.

God came up where they were hiding. He called out to Adam, "Adam, where are you?" Adam answered God, "I heard you coming through the Garden and I became frightened because I was naked, so I hid from you."

God looked at Adam and said, "Who told you you were naked? Did you eat fruit from the tree I told you not to eat from?"

TEACHER: Do you ever wonder how your parents know when you have done something wrong without you or someone else telling them? I know when I was your age, I used to wonder that very thing about my parents.

JENNIE: Again, God asked Adam, "Have you eaten from the tree I commanded you not to eat?"

Adam said, "Eve. She gave me the fruit from the tree and I ate it."

God turned to Eve and asked, "What did you do, Eve?" Eve then pointed at the snake and said, "The snake tricked me and I ate the fruit."

God took skins from some animals and made clothes for Adam and Eve to wear. He gave punishment to all three of them, Adam, Eve and the snake. God does not like sin. He cannot let it go unpunished. God was very sad with what happened. The next thing He did made Him even sadder. He made Adam and Eve leave the Garden. They could no longer live there.

TEACHER: You see kids, sinning is not a good thing at all. There is a very great price which must be paid. It breaks God's heart when we do whatever we want and do not obey Him in what He says we are to do or not do. But God is a just God. He is perfect. He cannot be in the presence of sin. That is why He sent His Son, Jesus Christ. He was born like you were. He grew up and became a man. But He never sinned. He did what was expected of Him by his parents and the leaders at the synagogue. But most of all He listened to what God, His father, told Him to do. Then, He was put on a cross and died for your sin and my sin. He is the way God planned it so we might be able to be in Heaven with Him forever, not just after we die but as we grow up and live our lives. He died in our place. When we ask God to forgive our sins and become our Lord, He will forgive us.

NOTES

NO LUNCH TODAY, BOYS!
Daniel 6:4-28

TEACHER: Today we are going to hear a story regarding a man who chose to obey God and follow Him at all costs. We are going to hear it from someone who has a first- hand account of this. His name is Raad. His name means thunder. When you meet him you will understand. (Some roaring can be heard. It is soft at first and then it grows louder. The teacher looks around with some concern.) (All of a sudden a lion is seen jumping through the curtain. It sits on the table next to the teacher and looks at the children. He sits and just stares at them. A few roars are given off.)

TEACHER: Welcome Raad. It is so good to have you join us today. Did you had a good journey ? Would you like some water perhaps?

RAAD: (ROAR!!!) NO! I want something to eat. I am famished. Are you tender to eat (he looks at one of the children on the front row).

TEACHER: No, Raad. These are the children who came to hear your story today. You promised to be on good behavior. Mind your manners!

RAAD: Ahhhh! I was just having some fun. I had a sandwich before I came in. I'm not hungry at all. Although, you look sweet enough to eat! (He looks at another one on the front row.) What about some dessert? Just kidding, just kidding!!

TEACHER: Well, Raad. Do you have something to tell us about what God did a long time ago? It was amazing, wasn't it?

RAAD: It was amazing. But before we get to the part where I am involved, I need to give you a little background. My name is Raad. That is Egyptian for thunder. That is because I roar so ferociously. ROAR!!!

Back a very long time ago, there was a king whose name was Darius. There was a governor or an officer whose name was Daniel. He stood out above the others because he was very capable and he had great ability. Darius did not miss how good Daniel was and he had started to make plans to move him up in position so he would be over the entire empire.

This was a very important step for Daniel and the other officers didn't miss the importance of it. They wanted very badly to find something wrong with Daniel so he would not appear to be so good to King Darius. They kept looking for anything that would put just a bit of doubt in the king's mind against Daniel. Guess what? They could not find anything. They looked to see if maybe he was not running the government affairs as they should be. He was doing a great job. They couldn't even find one single thing in his personal life to criticize or condemn. He was faithful, always responsible and completely trustworthy. There was nothing with which they could find fault in him.

After a time of talking amongst themselves, they decided the only way they could find anything by which to accuse him was in the rules of his religion.

TEACHER: They sound like they were very mean and dishonest men.

RAAD: They were. They continued to talk about this with each other. Finally, the other officers went before the king and said, "Long live King Darius! We all agree together that the king should make a law that be strictly enforced. Give orders that for the next thirty days any person who prays to anyone, some other god or human, except to you, your Majesty, will be thrown into the den of lions."

That is pretty serious stuff kids! ROAR!!! They knew because of Daniel's strong faith in his God that they would finally have him where they wanted him. OUT OF THE WAY!! (Raad begins to huff and growl just thinking of this.)

TEACHER: That must have been a terrible thing to watch happen! What did the king do?

RAAD: Well, the king was very egotistical. In other words, he thought way too much of himself. These men who came up with this plan for the new law did not think too much of the king. They did not have any respect for the king. They were thinking about what they wanted. They were using the king to do evil against Daniel. They knew that King Darius had a problem of thinking that he was the best and all should look up to him. And the king did just what they thought he would do.

King Darius listened as these men pumped him up and made him think that this would be a law to bring honor to him. He was so busy thinking about how good it sounded about him and that he would have popularity from all the people, he did not think what it would do to others, others for whom he had a great deal of respect. Namely Daniel. So Darius wrote out the decree. By a law made many years before by the first or ancient governments made it so whatever Darius wrote out as a law could not be repealed or replaced or changed in any way.

TEACHER: That was a very powerful piece of paper. It said that no one, including Daniel, could pray to their god. And if they did worship their god, they could be placed in the Lion's den. How do you think Daniel felt about this? How do you think you would feel about this? (Wait to get answers from the kids.) You would not be able to come to Sunday School, Children's church, or VBS. Would you like that?

RAAD: That would be awful. When Daniel heard that the law had been written and was put up on display, he went home. The men who wanted to trick Daniel went to Daniel's home and stood across the house where they could watch the window.

TEACHER: What do you suppose they were waiting for? (Give the children a chance to discuss and give some possible answers.)

RAAD: ROAR! I did not like these men. If I could have just had a moment out of my cage ..., I could have solved the problem. ROAR!

But it didn't seem to bother Daniel that a law had been written which said he could not pray to God. Daniel went into his upstairs room and went over to the window which opened toward Jerusalem. Without any delay and without thinking about it, Daniel got onto his knees and prayed to God. He gave thanks to Him just as before the law had been written. Not only did he do it that time, but he prayed in front of that window every day. And he didn't do it just once a day but he did it three times a day. In Psalm 55:17 it tells that King David prayed three times a day to God also.

TEACHER: We are told in Psalms in the Bible that King David prayed 3 times a day also. The Bible also tells us how we are to praise and worship God and how worthy He is of our praise and worship.

RAAD: These evil men did not waste any time. They had gone as a group to watch to see what they already knew Daniel would do.

TEACHER: These men, remember, knew how very faithful Daniel was to his God.

RAAD: The men saw Daniel praying 3 times a day everyday to his God. So they went to talk to King Darius about his decree or law.

EVIL MEN: Oh, mighty King Darius! Didn't you write a law declaring for the next 30 days that anyone who prays to any god or man, except you, O king, would be thrown into the lions' den?

KING DARIUS: The law stands --- according to the ancient governments. It cannot be repealed or changed.

EVIL MEN: Daniel is not paying attention to it at all. He continues to pray to his God 3 times a day. He does not pay attention to you or your law during this time of 30 days.

RAAD: (Strong huffing and low rumbling growls come from RAAD. King Darius liked Daniel very much and did not want him to suffer from a very foolish law he had made. He tried everything he could think of to save Daniel until sundown. Then once again the men came as a group before King Darius.

EVIL MEN: Oh King. Remember that the ancient governments state that no law that the king issues can be changed.

RAAD: So King Darius gave the order and Daniel was brought to the king's court and was thrown into the lions' den. As Daniel was being taken, King Darius called out to him, "Daniel, may your God, whom you serve continually, rescue you.

They sealed the mouth of the den with a great stone and the king pressed his signet ring into it.

TEACHER: A signet ring has a fairly flat surface on which is as specific design that represents the king. They would press this into wax and only the king could say when it could be broken. This was used instead of a signature as we use today.

RAAD: And just so there was no question about how serious this law was, all of the noble men to the king did the same with their rings.

With all of that done, the king returned to his quarters in the palace. He refused to have anything to eat, refused any entertainment all evening long. Finally he went to bed. But he could not sleep. He tossed and turned all night. All he could do was think of his friend Daniel. He did not sleep at all.

When the sun was just beginning to peak up over the eastern hills, King Darius got up and rushed to the lions' den, my home.

When he reached the den, he called out to Daniel in a very anguished voice.

KING DARIUS: Daniel, servant of the living God, has your God, whom you serve continually, been able to rescue you from the lions?"

RAAD: King Darius was very frightened that he had killed his friend Daniel because of a very selfish, foolish decision he had made.

DANIEL: O King, live forever! God, my God, had sent an angel to shut the lions' mouths. I have not been hurt. I don't even have a scratch on me. God found me to be innocent in His sight. And I have never done anything wrong before you, O king.

RAAD: King Darius was beside himself with happiness, joy and any other good feeling. He immediately ordered that Daniel be lifted out of the den. As they lifted Daniel up, they looked but no wounds could be found. God had saved Daniel. Daniel had trusted God. ROAR!

TEACHER: Was that the end of the story Raad?

RAAD: NO! The men who wanted to trick Daniel and be rid of him were standing behind the king with their eyes very large and their mouths wide open. They could not believe it. They had been so certain he would be found eaten by the hungry lions; but there he was being lifted without so much as a scratch to be seen.

Their presence did not slip the attention of the king. He then gave a final command that these evil men, their wives and their children were to be thrown down into the lions' den.

Were we ever hungry! My friends and I snagged our feasts before their feet felt the floor of the den. It was such a delectable meal.

TEACHER: (Visibly shudder so the children see.) My goodness, Raad. That is some story.

RAAD: But only if you disobey God or do not consider who He is. He will protect and save those who put their faith in Him as Daniel had done when he was a young boy. If you choose not to put your faith in Him, He will not save you. He will not take you to heaven with Him one day. Just remember ol' Raad and Daniel when you find yourself where you have to choose between God and people here on earth. God loved you enough to send His son. The people do not. They cannot help or save you nor will they. Just remember.

NOTES

ABOUT THE AUTHOR

Debbie Miley was saved at a small Baptist Church when she was in the ninth grade. She did not have any formal training in working with children or studying the Bible. At the age of 19 she worked with children in different areas continuing to the last few years. She has used her talents in teaching Awana, Pioneer Girls, VBS, Sunday School, and Children's Church. She always felt comfortable that this was the place she was to serve in the church. The Lord blessed her talent in working with children as she ministered under the guidance of a great pastor and very Godly mentors. Because of some health concerns her husband, Gary, encouraged her to retire early. The last few years the Lord has prompted her with ideas of writing of Sunday School programs and puppet skits. Her feelings are this book could be a vital tool in reaching children for Christ. Its use could also foster an opportunity for young people to serve within the church by developing a puppet ministry.

Matilda

Harley

Raad

Printed in the United States
By Bookmasters